MAR 2 1 2015

The Math of
Baseball

Ian F. Mahaney

PowerKiDS
press.

New York

For Brenda

Published in 2012 by The Rosen Publishing Group, Inc.
29 East 21st Street, New York, NY 10010

First Edition

Editor: Joanne Randolph
Designer: Greg Tucker

Photo Credits: Cover, pp. 4–5, 6–7, 13 (inset) Shutterstock.com; p. 8 (inset) Jeff Zelevansky/Getty Images; pp. 8–9 Scott Boehm/Getty Images; p. 10 (inset) J. Meric/Getty Images; pp. 10–11 Greg Flume/Getty Images; pp. 12–13 Paul Spinelli/MLB Photos via Getty Images; pp. 14–15 Christian Petersen/Getty Images; pp. 16–17 Nick Laham/Getty Images; p. 18 (inset) Jonathan Daniel/Getty Images; pp. 18–19 Photo File/MLB Photos via Getty Images; p. 20 (inset) Bob Levey/Getty Images; pp. 20–21 Focus on Sport/Getty Images.

Library of Congress Cataloging-in-Publication Data

Mahaney, Ian F.
 The math of baseball / by Ian F. Mahaney. — 1st ed.
    p. cm. — (Sports math)
 Includes index.
 ISBN 978-1-4488-2554-7 (library binding) — ISBN 978-1-4488-2692-6 (pbk.) —
ISBN 978-1-4488-2693-3 (6-pack)
 1. Baseball—Juvenile literature. 2. Baseball—Statistical methods—Juvenile literature. 3. Arithmetic—Juvenile literature. I. Title.
 GV867.5.M35 2012
 796.3570151—dc22
                                    2010026237
Manufactured in the United States of America

CPSIA Compliance Information: Batch #WW11PK: For Further Information contact Rosen Publishing, New York, New York at 1-800-237-9932

Contents

How Does Baseball Work?

In baseball, two teams play each other. The teams take turns playing **offense** and **defense**. The object of the game is to score more runs than the opponent, or other team.

The team on defense has nine players on the field. One of these defensive players is the pitcher. The pitcher throws the ball for the batter to hit. The batter is a member of the offense. Only one batter hits

The batter stands at home plate. If he gets a hit, he will run to first base. You can see first base here toward the top of the picture.

freecreditreport.com Know your Score:

State Farm

335'

at a time. The offense keeps sending players up to bat until the defense gets players on the offense out three times. Then the teams switch sides. Your math skills can help you learn more about the national pastime!

An inning is when each team gets a turn at bat. Each team gets three outs per inning. There are normally nine innings in a baseball game. How many outs are there in a normal game?

A) 2 outs x 9 innings = 18 outs
B) 3 outs x 9 innings = 27 outs
C) 6 outs x 9 innings = 54 outs

(See page 22 for the answers.)

Measuring the Field

There are two parts of the field. They are the infield and the outfield. The infield is the same size and shape on every field. There are four **bases** on the infield that sit 90 feet (27 m) apart from each other. If all four bases are the same distance from each other, what shape do they make? If you said "a square," then you are right.

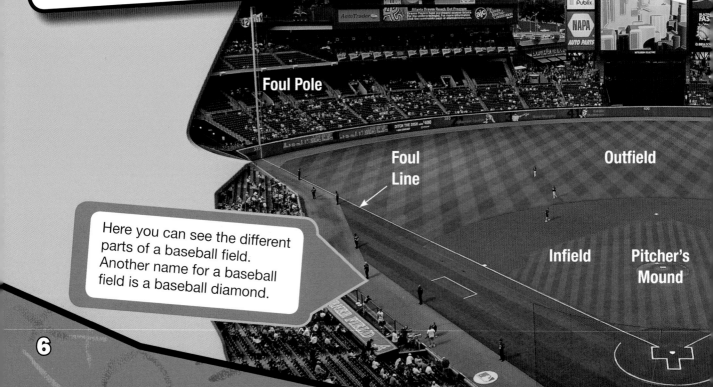

Foul Pole

Foul Line

Outfield

Infield

Pitcher's Mound

Here you can see the different parts of a baseball field. Another name for a baseball field is a baseball diamond.

In the middle of the square there is a pitcher's mound and a pitching rubber. The rubber is 60 feet 6 inches (18.4 m) from **home plate**. The pitcher keeps his foot on the rubber when pitching. The batter stands at home plate when hitting.

(See page 22 for the answers.)

Figure It Out!

In Little League, the field is smaller than a professional field. The bases are 60 feet (18 m) from each other. A home run is when a player hits the ball over the fence and scores a run. Let's say you hit a home run. You need to run around and touch all four bases. You start at home plate and run to first, second, and third base, then back to home plate. How far have you run?

Foul Pole

Foul Line

It's a Fact!

If a ball lands in the space between the foul lines, it is a fair ball. This means it is in play. If it lands outside the lines, it is foul, or out of play.

7

Balls and Strikes

The pitcher's job is to throw the baseball into a batter's strike zone. The strike zone is an imaginary box formed by the sides of home plate and the space between the batter's knees and chest. Sometimes the baseball is pitched into the strike zone, and the batter does

The space outlined in yellow here is the strike zone.

not hit it. This pitch is called a strike. If the baseball misses the strike zone, and the batter does not swing, it is called a ball.

When the pitcher throws four balls to a batter, the batter walks, or moves to first base. If the pitcher throws three strikes to a batter, the batter is out.

A batter tries not to swing at pitches he cannot hit. Pitchers try to trick the batter into swinging, though.

Figure It Out!

The number of balls and strikes a pitcher has thrown to a batter is called the count. The balls are listed first and the strikes second. If a pitcher has thrown the batter three balls in a row, then one strike, and the batter fouls off the fifth and sixth pitches, what is the count? (*Hint:* Be sure to read the sidebar before trying this one!)

(See page 22 for the answers.)

It's a Fact!

The batter can also hit foul balls. A foul is a ball that is hit outside the foul lines. When the batter hits a foul with fewer than two strikes, the foul counts as a strike. If the foul is hit when the batter already has two strikes, the foul does not count. The batter then gets to hit again.

What a Hit!

When the batter hits the ball, many things can happen. If one of the players on the field catches the ball in the air, the batter is out. The batter may hit the ball on the ground. If a fielder gets the ball and throws it to first base before the batter gets there, the batter is out.

Carl Crawford of the Tampa Bay Rays runs to make a catch in the outfield.

If the batter beats the ball to first base, the batter has hit a single. If the batter makes it to second base, the batter has a double. If the batter makes it to third, it is called a triple. If the batter runs around the bases and back to home before the ball gets there, the batter has hit a home run.

Figure It Out!

To calculate the number of hits a player has, add up the number of singles, doubles, triples, and home runs. In 2009, Ichiro Suzuki had 225 hits. He had 31 doubles, 4 triples, and 11 home runs. How many singles did he have?

(See page 22 for the answers.)

Here Ichiro Suzuki of the Seattle Mariners hits a single.

What Is Trajectory?

A ball hit by a batter can travel high in the sky or low near the ground. It can also travel fast, slow, or somewhere in between. It is the job of the fielders to judge the **speed** and **trajectory** of a baseball that is hit. The trajectory is the path that the ball takes in the air. A trajectory is always a curve.

Learning to watch the ball and judge where it is going are important skills for fielders. Fielders also listen to the bat connect with the ball. A sharp crack generally means the baseball will fly a long way!

This batter hit a line drive. Line drives stay low and close to the ground.

Figure It Out!

Look at these two examples of a trajectory a baseball could follow. Let's say that both balls were hit with the same force and speed. Which one do you think will end up farther away from home plate? Baseball players make judgments like these every time they are on the field!

(See page 22 for the answers.)

What a Pitch!

When a pitcher throws the ball, **coaches** and **managers** pay attention to the pitch's **velocity**. Velocity is how fast something moves over a distance.

The pitcher often throws the ball as hard as she can. A really fast pitch can be hard to hit! Other times, the pitcher knows the batter is looking for that fast pitch. Instead the pitcher throws a slower ball. When pitchers mix the types of pitches they throw to batters, the batter does not know what is coming. This makes it harder for batters to get hits. Coaches often look at the difference in velocities of the fast pitches and slower pitches to see how well a pitcher is doing.

Mariano Rivera of the New York Yankees can throw a fastball up to 96 miles per hour (154 km/h).

Figure It Out!

One of the most common slower pitches is a changeup. A changeup looks just like a fastball but is thrown with a weaker hold on the ball so its velocity is slower. Sam throws his fastball 82 miles per hour (132 km/h) and his changeup 74 miles per hour (119 km/h). What is the difference between the two velocities?

(See page 22 for the answers.)

The Standings

Most baseball teams play in a **league**. The teams are often put in a chart that is based on how often they win. This is called their winning **percentage**, though it is really an **average** not a percentage. A team's winning percentage is found by dividing the number of wins a team has by the number of games the team has played. If the San Francisco Giants have won four games and lost one,

It's a Fact!

The standings also list how far each team is from first place in a column labeled Games Back. To find this number, subtract the number of wins a team has from the wins of the first-place team. Next subtract the winning team's losses from the other team's losses. Add the two numbers together and divide by two. The result is the number of games back that team is from first place.

Here Ryan Howard of the Philadelphia Phillies plays in the 2009 World Series. This is the last series in the MLB play-offs.

A winning percentage is written as a decimal followed by three digits. Solve the problems below to find each team's winning percentage. Now put them in the correct order.

A) $8 \div 14 = ?$
B) $5 \div 12 = ?$
C) $6 \div 10 = ?$

(See page 22 for the answers.)

their winning percentage is $4 \div (4 + 1) = .800$. Winning percentages are normally rounded off to three decimal places.

The team with the highest winning percentage is ranked first. Everyone else follows in order, from highest to lowest. This is called the standings.

Hitting Statistics

Fans, coaches, and players like to study a hitter's **performance** to see how good a hitter is. To do this, we look at **statistics**. Statistics means the study and understanding of sets of numbers.

Basic hitting statistics count events. Counting events, such as home runs or hits, helps people understand how powerful or good a batter is.

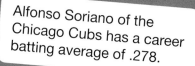

Alfonso Soriano of the Chicago Cubs has a career batting average of .278.

Ted Williams, who played for the Boston Red Sox, has one of the highest career batting averages in history.

In 1941, Ted Williams had 185 hits in 456 at bats. What was his batting average?

(See page 22 for the answers.)

Baseball fans also look at averages. The most common average fans look at for hitters is their batting averages. A batting average is found by dividing the number of hits by the number of at bats. It is shown with three decimal places.

Pitching Statistics

Like batters, pitchers have statistics, too. Fans often count the number of wins and the number of losses a pitcher has. If a pitcher has five wins and four losses, we say his record is five and four.

Tim Lincecum of the San Francisco Giants has a career ERA of 2.94.

It's a Fact!

A pitcher's record can also be written as a winning percentage. Using the numbers given above, you figure it out like this:
5 wins ÷ 9 games = .556.

The most important average for a pitcher is his **earned run** average, or ERA. An ERA shows us the average number of runs hitters could get from the pitcher if the pitcher pitched nine innings. We find it by multiplying the number of earned runs a pitcher gives by nine. Then we divide that product by the number of innings the pitcher has pitched.

So much in baseball can be understood using math. What else would you like to learn about?

Bob Gibson pitched for the St. Louis Cardinals in 1970.

Figure It Out!

Bob Gibson won an award called the Cy Young Award for being the best pitcher in his league in 1970. It was his second Cy Young Award. In 1970, Bob Gibson pitched 294 innings and gave up 102 earned runs. What was his earned run average?

(See page 22 for the answers.)

Page 5: The answer is C). Another way to show the math in this problem is:
3 outs x 2 teams = 6 outs. 6 outs x 9 innings = 54 outs. You could also write:
2 (3 x 9) = 54 outs.

Page 7: 4 x 60 feet = 240 feet. You could also figure this out using addition:
60 + 60 + 60 + 60 = 240 feet.

Page 9:

Pitch Number	Ball/Strike/Foul	Count
1	Ball	1 ball, 0 strikes
2	Ball	2 balls, 0 strikes
3	Ball	3 balls, 0 strikes
4	Strike	3 balls, 1 strike
5	Foul	3 balls, 2 strikes
6	Foul	3 balls, 2 strikes

Page 11: 225 hits – 31 doubles – 4 triples – 11 home runs = 179 singles.

Page 13: B) Because the path is straighter, this ball will land farther away from home plate.

Page 15: 82 miles per hour – 74 miles per hour = 8 miles per hour (13 km/h – 119 km/h = 13 km/h).

Page 17: A) 8 ÷ 14 = .571, B) 5 ÷ 12= .416, C) 6 ÷ 10 = .600. So C) has the highest winning percentage, followed by A) and then B).

Page 19: 185 ÷ 456 = .406. No baseball player since then has hit more than .400 for a season!

Page 21: His ERA = (102 earned runs x 9 innings) ÷ 294 innings = 3.12. The earned run average normally has two decimal places.

Glossary

average (A-vrij) A middle value of a group of numbers. It is found by adding the numbers and then dividing the sum by the number of numbers in the group.

bases (BAYS-ez) Squares where a runner can stay without being tagged out by the defense.

coaches (KOHCH-ez) People who direct players on a team.

defense (DEE-fents) The team trying to stop the other team from scoring.

earned run (ERND RUN) A run scored because a pitcher let a batter get a hit but not a run that happens after a fielder makes a mistake.

home plate (HOHM PLAYT) The base where the batter stands to hit.

league (LEEG) A group of teams that play one another.

managers (MA-nih-jerz) People in charge of the players and coaches on a baseball team.

offense (O-fents) The team trying to score runs.

percentage (per-SENT-ij) One part of 100.

performance (per-FAWR-ments) How well someone does something.

speed (SPEED) How quickly something moves.

statistics (stuh-TIS-tiks) The study and understanding of groups of numbers.

trajectory (truh-JEK-tuh-ree) The curved path an object takes in the air.

velocity (veh-LO-suh-tee) How fast something moves through space.

Index

Web Sites

Due to the changing nature of Internet links, PowerKids Press has developed an online list of Web sites related to the subject of this book. This site is updated regularly. Please use this link to access the list:
www.powerkidslinks.com/sm/baseball/